CATHOLIC TALES AND CHRISTIAN SONGS

THE GREATEST DRAMA EVER STAGED

STRONG MEAT

A collection of works

by

Dorothy Leigh Sayers

"Nowell, nowell, nowell, nowell,
A Catholic tale have I to tell,
And a Christian song have I to sing
While all the bells in Arundel ring."
H. BELLOC.

And forthwith he came to Jesus, and said, Hail, Master; and kissed Him. And Jesus said unto him, Friend . . .

JESUS, if, against my will,
I have wrought Thee any ill,
And, seeking but to do Thee grace,
Have smitten Thee upon the face,
If my kiss for Thee be not
Of John, but of Iscariot,
Prithee then, good Jesus, pardon
As Thou once didst in the garden,
Call me "Friend," and with my crime
Build Thou Thy passion more sublime.

Contents

CATHOLIC TALES AND CHRISTIAN SONGS

Desdichado

This is the Heir; come let us kill Him.

*Who is this that cometh up from the wilderness, leaning upon her Be-
loved?*

CHRIST walks the world again, His lute upon His back,
His red robe rent to tatters, His riches gone to rack,
The wind that wakes the morning blows His hair about His face,
His hands and feet are ragged with the ragged briar's embrace,
For the hunt is up behind Him and His sword is at His side, . . .
Christ the bonny outlaw walks the whole world wide,

Singing: "Lady, lady, will you come away with Me,
Lie among the bracken and break the barley bread?
We will see new suns arise in golden, far-off skies,
For the Son of God and Woman hath not where to lay His head."

Christ walks the world again, a prince of fairy-tale,
He roams, a rascal fiddler, over mountain and down dale,
Cast forth to seek His fortune in a bitter world and grim,
For the stepsons of His Father's house would steal His Bride from
     Him;
They have weirded Him to wander till He bring within His hands
The water of eternal youth from black-enchanted lands,

Singing: "Lady, lady, will you come away with Me,
Or sleep on silken cushions in the bower of wicked men?

For if we walk together through the wet and windy weather,
When I ride back home triumphant you will ride beside Me then."

Christ walks the world again, new-bound on high emprise,
With music in His golden mouth and laughter in His eyes;
The primrose springs before Him as He treads the dusty way,
His singer's crown of thorn has burst in blossom like the may,
He heedeth not the morrow and He never looks behind,
Singing: "Glory to the open skies and peace to all mankind."

Singing: "Lady, lady, will you come away with Me?
Was never man lived longer for the hoarding of his breath;
Here be dragons to be slain, here be rich rewards to gain . . .
If we perish in the seeking, . . . why, how small a thing is death!"

The Triumph of Christ

GOD met man in a narrow place,
And they scanned each other face to face.

God spoke first: "What ails you, man,
The you should look so pale and wan?"

Quoth man: "You bade me conquer harm
With no strength but this weak right arm.

"I would ride to war with a glad consent
Were I, as You, omnipotent."

God said: "You show but little sense;
What triumph is there for omnipotence?"

Said man: "If You think it well to be
Such a thing as I, make trial and see."

God answered him: "And if I do,
I'll prove Me a better Man than you."

God conquered man with His naked hands,
And bound him fast in iron bands.

Christk the Companion

WHEN I've thrown my books aside, being petulant and weary,
And have turned down the gas, and the firelight has sufficed,
When my brain's too stiff for prayer, and too indolent for theory,
Will You come and play with me, big Brother Christ?

Will You slip behind the book-case? Will you stir the window-curtain,
Peeping from the shadow with Your eyes like flame?
Set me staring at the alcove where the flicker's so uncertain,
Then suddenly, at my elbow, leap up, catch me, call my name?

Or take the great arm-chair, help me set the chestnuts roasting,
And tell me quiet stories, while the brown skins pop,
Of wayfarers and merchantmen and tramp of Roman hosting,
And how Joseph dwelt with Mary in the carpenter's shop?

When I drift away in dozing, will You softly light the candles
And touch the piano with Your kind, strong fingers,
Set stern fugues of Bach and stately themes of Handel's
Stalking through the corners where the last disquiet lingers?

And when we say good-night, and You kiss me on the landing,
Will You promise faithfully and make a solemn tryst:
You'll be just at hand if wanted, close by here where we are standing,
And be down in time for breakfast, big Brother Christ?

PANTAS ELKYSO

Be ye therefore perfect.

You cannot argue with the choice of the soul.

GO, bitter Christ, grim Christ! haul if Thou wilt
Thy bloody cross to Thine own bleak Calvary!
When did I bind Thee suffer for my guilt
To bind intolerable claims on me?
I loathe Thy sacrifice; I am sick of Thee.

They say Thou reignest from the Cross. Thou dost,
And like a tyrant. Thou dost rule by tears,
Thou womanish Son of woman. Cease to thrust
Thy sordid tale of sorrows in my ears,
Jarring the music of my few, short years.

Silence! I say it is a sordid tale,
And Thou with glamour hast bewitched us all;
We straggle forth to gape upon a Graal,
Sink into a stinking mire, are lost and fall . . .
The cup is wormwood and the drink is gall.

I am battered and broken and weary and out of heart,
I will not listen to talk of heroic things,
But be content to play some simple part,
Freed from preposterous, wild imaginings . . .
Men were not made to walk as priests and kings.

Thou liest, Christ, Thou liest; take it hence,
That mirror of strange glories; I am I;

What wouldst Thou make of me? O cruel pretence,
Drive me not mad with the mockery
Of that most lovely, unattainable lie!

I hear Thy trumpets in the breaking morn,
I hear them restless in the resonant night,
Or sounding down the long winds over the corn
Before Thee riding in the world's despite,
Insolent with adventure, laughter-light.

They blow aloud between love's lips and mine,
Sing to my feasting in the minstrel's stead,
Ring from the cup where I would pour the wine,
Rouse the uneasy echoes about my bed . . .
They will blow through my grave when I am dead.

O King, O Captain, wasted, wan with scourging,
Strong beyond speech and wonderful with woe,
Whither, relentless, wilt Thou still be urging
Thy maimed and halt that have not strength to go? . . .
Peace, peace, I follow. Why must we love Thee so?

The Wizard's Pupil

It was written with red and black ink, and much of it he could not understand; but he put his finger on a line and spelled it through. At once the room was darkened, and the house trembled. (OLD FAIRY TALE).

TIME like a sullen school-boy stands
Beside the Wizard's knee,
The book of life between his hands,
And spells out painfully
The crabbed Christ-cross row,
The Alpha and the O.

His grimy fingers slowly trace
Each odd, repellent sign
In a dull fear to lose the place;
His voice, with listless whine,
Drawls through the scheduled hour
The syllables of power.

While Zeta is so like to Xi
Small thought has he to spare
For what the screed may signify,
(The Wizard in His chair
Smiles, knowing ere He look
All that is in the book).

But sometimes ill and sometimes well,
Reluctant and perplexed,
He gropes and stammers through the spell
From one sound to the next;
And when the last is read
God's Word wakes the dead.

The Dead Man

ONE that had sinned against the light
Lay self-murdered under night.

There came three men and walked thereby,
And at the cross-roads saw him lie.

Said the first: "I say that this is sin,
And none may answer for him therein."

The second: "Nay, we should have seen to this;
His blood as the blood of Abel is."

The third: "It is but the common case,
The weak thing beaten in the race."

Said the second: "At length he has fall'n on sleep;"
"Now," said the first, "shall he learn to weep;"

But the third said: "If he should live again
'Twill be but as mist or a drop of the rain."

Said the third: "Well, well! let the body rest;
If soul there be, be it banned or blest."

But the second: "We'll call it 'mind unsound'
And let him be buried in holy ground."

The first said: "This is the best to do."
With his hand he hammered the ash-stake through.

Now, one was the devil, and one was good,
And One of the three had died on rood.

The Carpenter's Son

*And the cedar of the house within was carved with knops and open
flowers, . . . and he overlaid the cherubims with gold.*

I MAKE the wonderful carven beams
Of cedar and oak
To build King Solomon's house of dreams,
With many a hammer-stroke,
And the gilded, wide-winged cherubims.

I have no thought in My heart but this:
How bright will be My bower
When all is finished; My joy it is
To see each perfect flower
Curve itself up to the tool's harsh kiss.

How shall I end the thing I planned?
Such knots are in the wood!
With quivering limbs I stoop and stand,
My sweat runs down like blood . . .
I have driven the chisel through My hand.

The Drunkard

*And she ran and he ran till they came to the Bridge of One Hair, and
she got over but the giant couldn't.*
OLD FAIRY TALE.

*Fac me cruce inebriari
Et cruore Filii. POPE INNOCENT III.*

*If bodies delight thee, praise God for them.
S. AUGUSTINE.*

All things are lawful. S. PAUL.

Christ and the Stoic, walking; a crowd; a drunkard. Christ speaketh:

THAT drunkard, in the fading light
Capering along a lofty wall . . .
The crowd say, Stoic (they are right!):
"If he were sober, he would fall."

. . . So you fear visionary things?
Dream-miracles illustrious?
The splendours of strange, purple kings,
The pomps of Elagabalus?

Gold griffins and green malachite,
And vessels carved of porphyry?
Lest, stumbling to the left or right,
Like Elagabalus you die?

SAYERS

Vainly you know the pathway wide
Enough to walk, not more or less . . .
The gulf that holds you terrified
To be nought else than nothingness!

Cast down your eyelids; do not look
Where far, fantastic heavens gleam,
Merrier than any story-book
And madder than a madman's dream.

Your sober, calculating feet
Will fail you on the fearful ridge . . .
Go, plant them flatly in the street,
Leave Me alone to face the bridge,

Who on the small, sharp, single hair
Strung tight across the blank inane,
Run forth unfaltering, free from care,
Made drunken with My cup of pain.

Justus Judex

I judge no man.

*God sent not the Son into the world to judge the world, but that the
world should be saved through Him. He that believeth on Him is not
judged: he that believeth not hath been judged already, because he
hath not believed.*

THERE came three men of the latter age, and stood at Peter's gate,
And searched through all the courts of Heaven to find some advocate;
The Eternal Father shook His head: "I know not who they be . . .
I never have heard in all their heart one thought of love to Me.

"How sayest thou, Lady Mary, that wast the carpenter's wife,
Did they lose the vision of All that Is in the little cares of life?"
"Alas! alas! their hearts were barred from the hallowed, humble
        things . . .
I have no knowledge of them before Thee, King of kings."

The Father looked on all the Saints, from Paul to Magdalene,
That wit so well what a sinner is, from the sinners that they have been,
But every eye was casten down, and dumb was every lip,
The Saints know nothing of any man that scorns man's fellowship.

Then fear came over those flaccid men: "Thou wilt not damn us thus?
We led such pretty, delightsome lives . . . will no man speak for us?"
The Father furrowed His brow in doubt: "It may be there is one . . .
Canst Thou find aught to say for these, Prince Jesus, My meek Son?"

O then up rose Prince Jesus Christ, the fieriest Lord in Heaven,
His feet clear as the burning brass among the candles seven,

His words were swifter than edged swords, they were more sharp than
      wine:
"Though My Father and mother cast them off, I claim the men for
      Mine.

"How shall I saw I know not these, when these knew me so well,
They stormed all day on the doors of Heaven to drag Me out to hell?
They were blind to the banners and deaf to song, they drowsed beside
      the ships,
But the call of the Cross could startle them up with fury on their lips.

"They caught like babes with witless hands at the Babylonian beast;
They cast the cloak of their patronage on the blank creeds of the East,
Where God shrinks down to a shrivelling point, and all things shrink
      with Him;
They bowed to Amon-ra for a jest, to Isis for a whim;

"They called on the Dwellers beneath the Door, and knew not what
they did;
They filched the magic of ageless gods from the guarded pyramid;
They fashioned them bracelets of sacred jade, and brooches of
      scarab-wings;
They babbled the names unspeakable of strong and merciless Things;

"And they set the soft, fierce Cyprian in the chambers, and took
      no note
If the bond of Baal was on their breast, the phallus upon their throat;
But they hated and feared the crucifix, and they could not pass it by,
But thrust it forth with spitting and sneers, for they knew that I am I.

"I walk in the world in judgment, to sunder and not condemn;
There be none so sunk and sodden but I lay My hand on them,
And if yet in the palsied body one answering pulse can leap,
Whether to love or hatred, they are not dead but sleep.

"Therefore I swear, O Father and God, I swear by Thy mighty throne,
With the blood that was shed on Calvary I bought them for Mine own;
It shall dye them with shame and scarlet, it shall sear them as burning
      coals,

For they spilt and trampled it into the mire, and it shall save their
souls.

"Unbar the gates, good Peter, and for twice a thousand years
Let them writhe 'neath the rod of My pity and the insult of My tears,
Till hate is bound to the wheels of love, and sin is made My slave,
And I bring Mine own from the deep again, My dead back from the
      grave."

White Magic

*And while he sat there they saw a lady, on a pure white horse . . .
coming along the highway that led from the mound; and the horse
seemed to move at a slow and even pace . . . And he took a horse and
went forward. And he came to an open, level plain, and put spurs to
his horse; and the more he urged his horse, the further was she from
him. Yet she held the same pace as at first . . . "Lady," said he, "wilt
thou tell me who thou art?" "I will tell thee, Lord," said she. "I am
Rhiannon."*
THE STORY OF PWLL PRINCE OF DYVED.

LOOKING out of my window high
Sursum cor!
I saw a merry chase go by,
E sus le cor!
I saw the merry chase go by
Before the sun was in the sky--
Sursum corda, sursum cornua,
Up, hart and horn!

The quarry went upon an ass
Sursum cor!
That soft and slowly forth did pass,
E sus le cor!
So soft and slowly forth did pass
His little hoofs upon the grass,
Sursum corda, sursum cornua,
Up, hart and horn!

And smiting with the scourge and spur,
Sursum cor!

Came king and priest and labourer,
E sus le cor!
Both priest and king and labourer,
The queen with her ladies after her,
Sursum corda, sursum cornua,
Up, hart and horn!

They sweep beside the water-mill,
Sursum cor!
An hundred yards betwixt them still,
E sus le cor!
An hundred yards betwixt them still
As they come hunting round the hill,
Sursum corda, sursum cornua,
Up, hart and horn!

And they may ride till they crack their breath
Sursum cor!
To track that quarry down to death,
E sus le cor!
They never will ride down to death
The Wizard-Man from Nazareth,
Sursum corda, sursum cornua,
Up, hart and horn!

Lignum Vitae

And the leaves of the Tree were for the healing of the nations.

WHEN I am grown so weary, my hands can keep no hold
Of the heavy water of living, in its jar of mortal gold,
And it slips and spills in the ocean; then I shall sink to sleep
Beneath the boughs of Yggdrasil, where the sea-ways are deep,
Or peer from slumberous eyelids to see the smooth, black stem
Stretch up to the world's foundations, and know that it beareth them;
While dim through the roofs of water I shall hear, and hardly hear
How the birds of Bran the Blessed sing Aves all the year.
The waves of God will go over me, the waves and the great, green
     flood,
Where the ash-buds break to blossom in a red gleam like blood.
Yggdrasil, Yggdrasil! . . . the branches sweep and spread
Till the Tree of the whole world's sorrow shadows my dreaming head;
And never a wind comes near it, but the leaves swing quietly
Night and day to the swinging of the sea, of the salt sea.

Christus Dionysus

THERE are three gates to the city;
One is of gold, and one
Beaten of shining silver,
And one is like the sun.

By one, the laughing lovers,
By two, the quiet priests,
By three, the Lord of laughter
Rides to the vineyard feasts;

Young Dionysus
Crowned with the thorn and vine;
His feet and hands are red with blood,
His mouth is red with wine.

Dead Pan

At the hour of Christ's agony a cry of "Great Pan is dead!" swept across the waves in the hearing of certain mariners; and the oracles ceased. PLUTARCH.

For we know that the whole creation groaneth and travaileth together in pain until now.

I fill up on my part that which is lacking of the afflictions of Christ.

AND there was darkness all over the land
Three hours; and in the dark so wild a cry
That all men hearing sought to understand
What thing it was that in such pain must die.

But there was darkness, so that none may say
What there befel, except the midnight bird
Whose staring face is still struck white to-day
For blank amaze at all he saw and heard.

He that maintained unblinded vigil there
Told us: "There were vast shapes which loomed and grew
Around, and He was fearfully changed: I swear
They were goat's feet the nails had stricken through.

"How mourned pale Isis, 'neath the hideous rood
Crouched in the dust! How passed in one fierce sound
Side-smitten Balder! For what grim festal food
Smoked forth the blood of Mithra to the ground?

"But Pasht my cousin, the wise African,
Looked from the judgment hall toward the North,
And knew all things fulfilled when thus began
The deathless Ritual of the Coming Forth;

"For One came treading those eternal floors
That was the Word of the tremendous Book,
Crying throughout the long-drawn corridors
So that the porters of the pylons shook:

"I am Osiris! and the gates reeled back
Before the God twin-crowned with white and red,
And an echo rose and went in the wind's track
Over the Middle Sea: Great Pan is dead! . . .
Whereat the oracles fell mute," he said.

Rex Doloris

*Signed with the sign of His Cross and salted with His salt. S.
AUGUSTINE.*

"WHEREFORE wilt thou linger, Lady Persephone?
The sheaves are gathered, the vintage is done,
Bacchus through the ivy leaves laughing with his satyrs
Calls us to the feasting, and the ripe, red sun
Drops like an apple, tumbling to the westward,
The shout of the Maenads is merry on the hill,
Why do the wheat-ears fall from thy fingers?
Whom does thou look for, lingering still?

"Whom dost thou look for? Here is one to woo thee,
Brown-cheeked, beautiful, lissom as the larch,
Lightsome, slender, blossomy with kisses,
Merrier-footed than the winds in March;
Loose thy hair to dream along his shoulder,
Drowse in thy whiteness warm upon his breast,
He shall feed thee with wheaten cakes and honey
And all fair fruits that are rich and daintiest."

"I weary of the feast, I weary of the harvesting,
I weary of your music, children of the earth--
Your feet dance over the roofs of my palaces,
The halls of Hades ring hollow to your mirth;
The great King of Grief hath reft me, ravished me,
Broken me with kisses, conquered me with pain,
I have drunk his bitter wine, I have eaten of His pomegranates,
Can find no savour in the honeycomb again."

"Wherefore wilt thou linger, Lady Persephone?
When sheaves are gathered and the vintage is done,
And Bacchus through the ivy leaves laughing with his satyrs
Calls us to the feasting, and the ripe, red sun
Drops like an apple, tumbling to the westward,
While the shout of the Maenads echoes from the hill?"
"Ere the round moon rise ruddy on the corn-shocks
The Lord of Hades shall have me at His will."

Sacrament

AGAINST ECCLESIASTS.

BETWEEN the Low Mass and the High,
Between the Altar and my cell,
I met Christ and passed Him by,
And now I go in fear of Hell.

My dying brother Ninian
Confessed himself to me and said:
"I find the Christ in every man,
But how comes He in wine and bread?"

I cursed my brother as he died,
"Absolvo" I would not repeat,
I bare away the Crucified,
I would not sign his breast and feet.

I lifted Christ above my head,
I kneeled to Him, I bare Him up,
And Christ cried to me from the bread,
Christ cried upon me from the cup:

"What is this bitter sin of thine,
So little to have understood, . . .
To find Me in the bread and wine
And find Me not in flesh and blood?

"Go, say thy Mass for Ninian,
That, when he comes to Heaven, maybe

His prayer shall save thee, righteous man . . .
If he can find the Christ in thee!"

Sion Wall

He that hath an ear, let him hear what the Spirit saith to the churches.

AS I was walking by Sion wall
A wonder sight I came to see,
And that was Peter and John and Paul
Casting the dice by Calvary tree.

"What is this game that ye have found,
Peter and Paul and fair, sweet John?
O lift your eyes a little from the ground
And see what ye shall look upon.

"O Mother, Mother, ease My head,
O set thy hand against My back; . . .
So many years and I am not dead
But rive in sunder on the rack.

"I am full weary of My groans,
I weep so fast, I cannot see,
My children gamble with dead men's bones,
And I may count the bones of Me.

"Now rede Me, Mother, and rightly rede,
What is this game, and what the stake?" . . .
"My dear, they play for the seamless weed
I wove so whitely for Thy sake.

"They cast the dice by six and three,
They cry a match, they call a main,

They have no time to pause and see
How Thou art crucified again."

"O leave your game," St. Maudleyn said,
"And let the robe be whose it list,
But loose the hands that blessed my head,
Set free the feet that I have kissed."

As I walked by Sion wall
A wonder sight was in mine eyes,
How that Peter and John and Paul
By Calvary tree sat, casting dice.

Byzantine

Jesus Christ, the same yesterday and to-day and for ever.

I SIT within My Father's house, the Lord God crucified,
My feet upon the altar-stone set straitly side by side,
My knees are mighty to uphold, My hands outstretched to bless,
My eyelids are immutable to judge unrighteousness.

What though the bitter winds of war lay waste the house of prayer?
They cannot shake My quiet robe nor stir My folded hair,
I wrestled in Gethsemane, I cried and I was slain,
Never, for any strife of men, to strive nor cry again.

I sit within My Father's house, with changeless face to see
The shames and sins that turned away My Father's face from Me;
Be not amazed for all these things, I bore them long ago
That am from everlasting God, and was and shall be so.

Epiphany Hymn

Nations shall come to Thy light and kings to the brightness of Thy rising.

LORD CHRIST, and have we found Thee then, Desire of all the ages,
In fashion as the woman's Seed, conceived and born of her?
Behold Thy pilgrims, mighty Child, and smile upon the sages
That from so far a land have brought their incense, gold and myrrh.

To Thee, to Thee, through countless years of blind and bitter groping,
The reek of sacrifice went up beneath the idols' feet,
To Thee the piteous prayers of men, in trembling and in hoping,
That satest in the hill of Jove, and in Osiris' seat.

From all the hearts that learned to love and look for no rewarding,
Still faithful to the best they knew, and were not bought nor sold,
From all dim dreams of holiness beyond the world's affording,
With toil and sweat was hammered out Thy kingly crown of gold.

White is Thy bearing-cloth, but Thou shalt have a red arraying
With blood of all that bare Thy pain, and knew not what they bare,
Thy stripes and shames and agonies, Thy wounds and guiltless
    slaying,
The hemlock and the myrrh are Thine, the gall and vinegar.

Arise, O Orient Splendour, rise and shine to all men living,
From east and west their cry is heard, their very instant cry,
Arabia, Saba, Tharsis kneel, their richest treasures giving,
Stand forth, O Jesus, justified in Thine Epiphany.

Carol

THE Ox said to the Ass, said he, all on a Christmas night:
"Do you hear the pipe of the shepherds a-whistling over the hill?
That is the angels' music they play for their delight,
'Glory to God in the highest and peace upon earth, goodwill' . . .
Nowell, nowell, my masters, God lieth low in stall,
And the poor, labouring Ox was here before you all."

The Ass said to the Ox, said he, all on a Christmas day:
"Do you hear the golden bridles come clinking out of the east?
Those are the three wise Mages that ride from far away
To Bethlehem in Jewry to have their lore increased . . .
Nowell, nowell, my masters, God lieth low in stall,
And the poor, foolish Ass was here before you all."

Fair Shepherd

FAIR Shepherd must weep
He has lost His sheep
And cannot tell where to find them;
Far from their home
They wander alone
And never will look behind them.

He lay by night
In His chamber bright
And dreamed He saw them dying,
And when He awoke
His heart it was broke,
For He heard them still a-crying.

Then up He took
His staff and crook,
Determined for to find them;
He found them indeed
But they gave Him no heed
And cast His words behind them.

He was haled away
On a Good Friday
To Calvary Hill hard by,
Mocked and denied,
Struck through the side
And hung on a Tree to die.

Through death and hell
He searched as well,

And still in the world doth roam;
He hath done what He could,
As a fair Shepherd should,
To bring His lost sheep home.

A Song of Paradise

SING a song of Paradise
Far above the skies,--
Four-and-twenty Elders
And Monsters full of eyes!
Heaven's gates are opened,
They all begin to sing,
Playing ball with golden crowns
Round about the King.

The King is in His counting-house,
Counting His elect,
The Queen comes from her chamber
Royally bedecked
With chrysoprase and amethyst
And jacinth without price . . .
Now is not this a pretty song
To sing of Paradise?

Carol for Oxford

WHEN all the Saints that are in Heaven keep Christmas at the board,
Our Lady Mary calls a health before her Son our Lord,
Says: "Let us sing the fairest town that is in all Your earthly crown;
Nowell, Nowell, Nowell, Nowell
To the Bells of Oxenford!"

Then saith the Holy Trinity: "There be We well adored;"
Saith John to Mary Maudleyn, "There we walk across the sward;"
And All the Souls that lived on earth lift up their voice to swell that
     mirth:
"Nowell, Nowell, Nowell, Nowell
To the Bells of Oxenford!"

King Jesus saith: "That will I well, thereof rest you assured
, For I have a dwelling fair and Church with aisles so broad;
So let us drink at Christmas time to all that dwell by Great Tom chime:
Nowell, Nowell, Nowell, Nowell
To the Bells of Oxenford!"

The Mocking of Christ

A MYSTERY.

O My people, what have I done unto thee, or wherein have I wearied thee? Testify against me.
THE REPROACHES.

So man made God in his own image.
THE BOOK OF GENESIS (adapted).

A HALL.

PERSONA DEI:
> I AM God Who all men made,
> And in human form obeyed,
> Till at last I was betrayed
> To hand of wicked men;
> They have judged Me now to die
> And prepare to crucify . . .
> Yet I will save their souls thereby
> And soon shall rise again.
> See now how these make mock of Me!
> They have not so much charity
> To leave Me to My grief . . .
> But they shall crown Me as their King
> And work full many a hateful thing,
> And never a one of them shall bring
> To Me the least relief.
> How have I merited, say, how,
> That on this wise they use Me now

Who did them so much good?
Have I not visited My vine
That it should give Me gall for wine?
Who then hath understood?
But see, these soldiers now draw near
To bruise and buffet, gibe and jeer
And hale Me to the rood.

FIRST SOLDIER:
Say brothers, what thing shall we do
Until this judgment be gone through?
We must make some good sport.

SECOND SOLDIER:
Let's dice.

THIRD SOLDIER:
I have too thin a purse.

FIRST SOLDIER:
Drink.

SECOND SOLDIER:
Why, the wine's as thin.

THIRD SOLDIER:
Aye, worse.

SECOND SOLDIER:
And here's a prisoner twice as thin . . .
I'll tell you what we shall begin.

ALL:
What's that?

SECOND SOLDIER:
We'll play now in this hall
At: Jesus Christ is Lord of all.

ALL:

> Well thought on! Fair and finely hit!
> Come on! We'll make the prisoner "It" . . .
> Here is a chair for Him to sit.

> *They set Christ in the centre and go out. They return, in or-*
> *der, dancing and mumming. All sing the chorus, dancing*
> *about the chair.*

POPE:

> Here come I with a robe of red
> And a crown to adorn His head,
> The key of heaven, the key of hell,
> And the world's treasure-house as well.

> *He setteth the robe upon Him, thrusteth the tiara over His*
> *eyes, and giveth Him three keys.*

CHORUS:

> Let us sing, whate'er befall:
> Jesus Christ is Lord of all.

> *They bow the knee.*

EMPEROR:

> Here's a crown of another style,
> Sword and sceptre for His hands,

> *He giveth temporal crown, sword and sceptre.*

POPE:

> Lest He use them though, meanwhile
> Tie Him up with fetter-bands.

> *They fetter Him.*

CHORUS:

> Let us sing, whate'er befall:
> Jesus Christ is Lord of all.

They bow the knee.

KING:

> I am on Tom Tiddler's ground, *etc.*,
> Picking up gold and silver.

POPE:

> Hence, begone thou scurvy swine,
> Gold and silver all are mine.

> *Pope and King run together and fight. They dodge about the chair. Their blows miss each other and fall upon Christ. They dance back to back and separate.*

KING:

> Black and white, black and white,
> Parchment is a pretty sight;
> Who keeps quiet and serves the King
> Can't go wrong in anything.

> *He binds a charter upon Christ's mouth.*

CHORUS:

> Let us sing, whate'er befall:
> Jesus Christ is Lord of all!

> *They bow the knee to Christ and to King.*

PREACHER:

> Here's a better crown,
> Here's a better gown,
> Pull the old ones down.

> *He putteth upon Christ a black gown and a shovel hat.*

> Take good heed and look
> You still speak by the Book . . .
> Never say a word
> But what we've always heard.

He setteth a Bible in His hand.

CHORUS:
>Let us sing, whate'er befall:
>Jesus Christ is Lord of all.

Here the people shall not bow the knee, but pull off their hats.

BISHOP:
>In respectable gaiters which button up tight
>He might walk in the precincts on Sunday,
>While His innate good taste will remind Him it's quite
>Shocking form to be found there on Monday.

He setteth upon Christ a bishop's apron and gaiters.

CHORUS:
>Let us sing, whate'er befall:
>Jesus Christ is Lord of all.

They bow the knee

CATHEDRAL ORGANIST:
>Sire, if You should wish to speak
>At any moment of the week,
>Kindly hit a decent A . . .
>(Plagal Amens I will play);
>Here we use the Magdalen Psalter . . .
>No, I see no cause to alter.

He placeth a psalter in Christ's hand, and conducts the singing of the chorus.

CHORUS:
>Let us sing, whate'er befall:
>Jesus Christ is Lord of all.

They bow the knee.

FIRST CURATE:
> *He setteth a tea-cup in Christ's hand.*
> Gossip and tea! gossip and tea!
> Communicants' class at a quarter-past-three.
> Oh dear! Mrs. Kidgup smells strongly of gin,
> And this is God's house . . . no, she must not come in!
> Magdalen? Yes, yes, but that's in the Bible,
> And a quite special case . . . if it wasn't a libel.

CHORUS:
> Let us sing, whate'er befall:
> Jesus Christ is Lord of all.

> *They bow the knee.*

SECOND CURATE:
> *He giveth Christ a cricket-bat and pads, and beateth Him*
> *boisterously upon the back.*
> Here we are again, hurray!
> Keep your shoulders square and play!
> That's the way that heaven is won . . .
> Well hit my lad! Again, Sir . . . run!

CHORUS:
> Let us sing, whate'er befall:
> Jesus Christ is Lord of all.

> *They bow the knee.*

RESPECTABLE GENTLEMAN:
> Hail, our Chairman of Committee,
> Much respected in the city!
> Tied up tight He will not irk us! . . .
> Now we'll regulate the workhouse.

> *They dance about Christ and wind Him up in red tape.*

CHORUS:
> Let us sing, whate'er befall:
> Jesus Christ is Lord of all.

They bow gravely.

PATRIOT:
> The Son of God goes forth to war
> A kingly crown to gain . . .
> We'll rake in something less or more
> By following in His train.

He setteth on Him a helmet.

CHORUS:
> Let us sing, whate'er befall:
> Jesus Christ is Lord of all.

They salute Him soldierly.

PATRIOT OF ANOTHER NATIONALITY:
> That helmet's not the proper sort . . .
> Makes Him look like poor old Jah . . .
> To be a modern God He ought
> To wear such weapons as mine are.

He setteth on Him a helmet of another fashion.

CHORUS:
> Let us sing, whate'er befall:
> Jesus Christ is Lord of all.

The Patriots squabble and spit on each other and on Christ.

SENTIMENTAL PERSON:
> Gentle Jesus mild and meek
> Smooth Your hair down neat and sleek;
> I am sure You did not say:
> "Tasteless salt is cast away" . . .
> Jesus, that would never do,

Or what *would* become of You?

He parts Christ's hair in the middle.

CHORUS:
    Let us sing, whate'er befall:
    Jesus Christ is Lord of all.

They bow the knee.

A MUMMER:
    Ho! stand away there! form a ring about!
    Here comes the King of Fools with all his rout.

Cometh in a Higher Critic, habited as the Roy des Sotz, with his masque.

DIONYSUS: (On an ass, with Fauns and Bacchae.)
    Dionysiacs you've heard of . . .
    Centuries cannot disperse us,
    Crown Him, crown Him, pluck His beard off
    And invest Him with the thyrsus.
    Though His priests and flock despise us,
    Still He's only Dionysus,
    Riding high on the twin asses
    Ere the summer solstice passes.

He plucketh Christ by the beard and setteth the thyrsus in His hand.

OSIRIS:
    Bring hither the white crown and the red
    For Him that is Lord of the North and the South,
    Risen quick from the land of the dead,
    The lotus-lily in His mouth . . .
    His Name is life in the courts of hell
    And the porters know that Name right well.

He giveth Him the red crown and the white, and a lotus flower.

ELIJAH:

> He does not look very like me, but they say we are the same . .
> And in any case you'll know it by the likeness of the name,
> Yes, for Jesus and Elijah must be forms of the same name.

JOSHUA:

> Pardon me, I think you're wrong . . .
> The resemblance is not strong.
> Joshua and Jesus clearly
> Are the same . . . or very nearly.
> He puts out the sun and moon,
> I can stop the sun at noon.
> Two can't play at such a game,
> Obviously we're the same.

ELIJAH:

> Never mind, let's both agree
> That I am you and you are me!

> *They crown Him with rays of the sun.*

GAUTAMA:

> I must beg that you will listen for a little moment, while
> I point out that this is Buddha (though debased and poor in
>> style);
> I was tempted; He was tempted; other men have been so too,
> And there was not much in common in the struggles we went
>> through;
> Then His Mother was a virgin, mine was married, so you see
> There's no difference between us . . . like as peas in pod are
> we.

> *He giveth Him the emblems of Buddha.*

MITHRA (solemnly):

> The Lord of fire!
> No man knoweth
> My mystical rite,
> Though many aspire.
> When the Sun showeth
> His forehead crowned with light

I am there, wonderful!
And the groaning, death-stricken bull
Bleeds for my sacrament.

He throweth a bull's hide about Christ.
Many a hidden thing
To my mysteries went.
My priests are fallen,
Fallen and slain . . .
O I the sorrowful King!
So 'tis befallen.

Briskly, with a change of tone.

This only is distinctly plain:
Whatever rites were practised at my shrine,
His must be imitations based on mine.
PRIEST OF THE GROVE OF NEMI:
"The priest who slew the slayer and shall himself be slain,"

He giveth Him a knife.
GREEN PERSON:
The spirit of vegetation that renews the crops of grain,

He giveth Him a garland and sickle.
BACCHAE:
The orgies of Eleusis . . .

They give Him the Phallic cones and emblems.
BALDER:
Balder struck dead . . .
PROMETHEUS:
Prometheus bringing fire from Heaven . . .

He giveth Him a torch.
ADONIS:
Adonis' sacred Bread.

He giveth a wafer.
ALL (dancing):

We're not alike to look at, but you may be satisfied
That we're each and all the one
  unmistakeable
  unadulterated
   primitive
   unsophisticated
   admirable
   rational
    spiritual
    proved
     accredited
and thoroughly homogeneous original of Jesus crucified!

CHORUS:
     Yes, we'll sing, whate'er befall:
     Jesus Christ is Lord of all!.

     They bow the knee.

PLATO:
     Pol Hercle, what a noise! and if you please
     Give me the credit of my own invention.

SOCRATES:
     My son, I do not wish to breed dissension
     But . . . did you never hear of Socrates?

     To Christ.
     Hemlock, sir, is a far genteeler fashion
     Of quitting life than is a gallows-passion.

     Offering hemlock.

PLATO (eagerly):
     That's where you're wrong. The righteous man, say I,
     Must die in shameful torment . . .

VOICE WITHIN:
     Crucify!

A CAPTAIN:

>What folly's this? Go, shift the prisoner straight;
>Bring Him to Golgotha without the gate.

>*They put on Him His own robe.*

PERSONA DEI:

>Now that I must come to die
>Nought is left of Me, save I
>Discrowned, stript, alone;
>Yet when I am lifted high
>I will cause all men draw nigh
>Unto My royal throne.
>As I go to Golgotha
>My tread shakes the earth afar.
>My voice shall sound at Heaven's bar,
>"Eloi, eloi, lama,
>Lama sabachthani."

>When My arms are stretched out
>They shall reach the world about,
>The round earth hangs upon My stout
>And stark and bitter Tree.
>Therefore all ye that go by
>Look and see how I hang high,
>If you may find the time to sigh:
>"Eleison Christe."

EXPLICIT.

The House of The Soul: Lay

I.

I HAVE forgotten my name and the name of my nation . . . yea,
I know alone I have lost myself, and have wandered far astray
From the land where the magical fir-trees grow, farther than far
    Cathay,
Farther than fair Atlantis or the hills of Tir-fa-tonn,
Or the isles of Bran and Mailduin, or the isle of Avalon;
From the city built on the rivers, where the willow-branches sway
To a quiet tune all night to the moon, and dream in the sun all day,
Where the gardens drink at the water's brink and the poppies dip to
    the water wan,
And the roses fall from the hot red wall like showers of light on the
water grey.

Now and again by night, when the sun's last ray
Has crawled under the sky-line, and I hear the waves' array
March clip-clap after me, driving me up the bay
That is ringed with cliffs and foam-girt, and the bats wheel out
    anon,
Sometimes I half remember . . . and again the word is gone;
And I know that I am lonely, and the night and the sea and the
    spray,
Unrestingly, unhastingly, march on with no delay,
And the sheer height of the cliffs' white sands like the base of the
    great white throne,
And I seem to be left with God, bereft of any wisdom to plead or
    pray.

SAYERS

II.

Some one has leased me a house that is huge and dark and old
And filled with other men's dust;
I do not remember bargaining, but I pay the price in gold,
Year after year . . . a heavy price . . . and pay it because I must.
Its rafters are full of mould
And its bars, of rust;
The slates fly from the roof at every gust
Of the wind over the wold.

I should like to search my house, if only I were bold,
And scrape the mildew-crust
From cobweb-curtained corners that are quaintly-shaped and cold
And heaped with curious hangings; yet I have but little lust
To find what may not be told
Or ever discussed
Hid in a closet, maybe, or carefully thrust
Into a curtain's fold.

III.

I am afraid of my house, and I wish I knew
Who
Those other tenants were
That my landlord leased it to;
I know that they have been there,
For sometimes I find a shoe
Or a ribbon for the hair . . .
There's a grandfather clock on the stair,
And an odd little bust on a bracket, for which I don't very much care.

"They have left long since; what matter to you?" . . .
True.
But I wish my house was bare
And perfectly clean and new,
For the hollowed seat of a chair
Or a rod wrenched askew
Gives me the creeps, and I dare
Hardly breathe in an air
So thick with the dust of those who once were here, and who now are
        . . . where?

IV.

One day the storm was loud, the clouds clung thick and red
Close to the windows, the sky glowed like a copper pan,
The thunder muttered and cracked, the lightning leapt from its bed
Like a beast, the rain ripped down like a curtain of iron thread;

And every nook of the house was dim and strange and dread,
And odd things shuffled and squeaked in the corners, and queer
    feet ran
Hither and thither . . . the light was split, furled and unfurled like a fan
. . .
That was a day of God's ban.

And it suddenly came to my mind that the house was inhabited
By people that hid themselves, and I swore to seek and scan
And find those flittering feet, and the voices, and what they said;
But the lightning flashed and shook me, and dizzied all my head,
And I searched each room and closet, and I sped and sped and sped
Through turret and tower and corridor, till trembling I began
To open the dungeon doors, and lo! in the deepest, an old, old man
That sat, and sang, and span.

V.

And, do you know, I could not find him again!
Not once! Though I sometimes fancied I heard a strain
With a sort of humming refrain;
And I'd tip-toe down the staircase, close to the wall
To deaden my footfall;
And the singing would rise and wane,
And the flame of my secret candle shrink, and shoot up smoky
    and tall.

So, very quietly creeping, I'd suddenly gain
A little, low, iron-bound door, and "Not in vain
This time," I would whisper, "my pain!"
Then I'd fling the door back quick with a cheery call . . .
Silence, nothing at all!
Now is it not wholly plain
That here was something of wizardry, mystical, magical?

VI.

I hate the clock;
It first says Tick,
It then says Tock;
I hear days flick,
I see years flock,
The whole world rock;
Had I the trick
I'd like to lock
Time with a block
To make it stick.

Hic, haec, and hoc,
Hoc, haec, and hic,
Each, at each knock
Drop likes a brick,
Sticks like a stock
Just at the shock
Caught in the nick;
Therefore the mock
Of that red cock
Turned Peter sick.

VII.

My house upon the landward side
Looks out toward the town;
Pleasant it is all day to bide
High in the thin air rarified,
And gaze delighted down
On busy folk that drive and ride
And run and crawl and hop and stride
Like beetles black and brown.

Stiff soldiers stalk, kings pace in pride,
And statesmen stoop and frown,
The women strut and mince and glide,
Priests bustle round at Eastertide, . . .
All but their boots their broad hats hide,
The wind blows out their gown, . . .
Tramps slouch and spit, boys jump and slide,
They look all head. How I deride
King, lady, priest and clown!

VIII.

My house is haunted and hell-enchanted by a conjuror vaunted . . .
hear them tripping,
Chattering, scattering, imps undaunted, here they come battering, pat-
tering, skipping,
Dancing and prancing, gloating and glancing, bawling, brawling, leer-
ing, and lipping,
Snarling and nipping
Clinging and gripping
Winding and whirling, twisting and twirling, sliding and sprawling
askew and slipping . . .

And they revel, vitriolic,
Diabolic,
Like a devil with the colic . . .
Topping! ripping!

O the smashing and O the crashing, O the hashing and slashing and
snipping
My goods! . . . If I could give you a thrashing, send you home with a
good sound whipping,
Bestial brood of a brutal mood, when the devil and I lay kissing and
clipping . . .
Now curtseying, dipping,
Sweating and dripping,
Heel-and-toeing, to-and-froing, winking, blinking, bibbing and sipping
. . .
How you frolic alcoholic,
How you rollick,
Me, a wretched melancholic,
Shaming, stripping!

IX.

This was the song that, like a distant bell
Exceeding light and thin,
Came at the dawning after nights of hell
From far away within;
Maybe from that unsearchable dark cell
It did begin
Where that old man, whose name I cannot tell,
Doth sit and spin.

"Empty the winds that can the clouds dispel,
And silence after din,
Water has virtue heats of wine to quell,
Fatigue gives pause to sin,
And rest seemed good to Adam when he fell,
As to his kin;
O well it is for me, O well, O well
This way to win."

X.

Yesterday, looking through my window-bars,
The whole sad sea was changed resplendently
By one great ship that sailed with raking spars
Into the sunshine; and her masts were three,
Red, splendid banners in the wind flew free,
Her blown white sails were thick with tempest-scars,
Twelve blazoned shields along her sides had she,
And round about her prow, the name of the Trinity.

By night she lit her lanterns from the stars
And on her decks held mighty jubilee
With wine poured out from strange Assyrian jars
And wheaten bread for all her company.
"O sirs," I cried, "whither with such good glee
Sail ye for merchandise or mighty wars?"
The Captain said: "Come down, take ship with me." . . .
Then with this song we weighed and sailed across the sea.

XI.

"We that speed on the shifting floor
Where the green waters vary
With many a song and stroke of oar,
Sail for the chase of the silver boar
That's horned and hoofed and hairy:
His eyes are bright, his bristles hoar,
And hung with golden bells galore;
O many a time he flees and flies across the uplands airy,
And fierce he is, and fleet he is, and light and wight and wary,
And bravely famed in faery lore
By many a hunter sought of yore.

"The dark, salt sea is bitter and frore,
The wind of comfort chary,
But though the drenching sleet downpour
And Manawyddan's green steeds roar,
We are not solitary,
For Rhiannon's green song-birds soar
About our heads for evermore.
With the first stroke for Jesus King, the second stroke for Mary,
The third stroke for the Trinity, the fourth for the land of faery,
By one, by two, by three, by four,
We reach the wonderful, weirded shore."

XII.

I am sailing to seek my name and the name of my nation
        . . . nay,
For I know the land that bore me, where the marvellous
        sea-beasts play,
Where are silver bells on the blackthorn boughs, and golden
        bells on the may,
Where the magical Boar abideth, and the birds of Rhiannon,
And Adam and Eve and Enoch, and Arthur and Prester John.
I have learnt the name of my city, and learnt to ask my way,
And the whole ship's crew are my fellows too, and a merry crew
        be they;
All day we sail with a favouring gale or gird ourselves as the
        storm draws on,
And strive and cope and rudder and rope, and sing aloud in the
        loud affray.

And other things I have learnt, and the first is still to say
To myself, "O unlearned fool!" and also, "Fool, be gay!"
O well for the glorious chase of God, and well for the hot assay!
Well for the noise of water, for the hills where the sun has shone,
For the trees on the far horizon and the chart we may not con!
Well for the terrible mer-wolf, and the caves where the witch-wife lay
Till we touched her brows where the fir-trees stand and all we witless
        wanderers wonne!
God bless the fools and the wise in schools, et gloria tibi, Domine!

THE GREATEST DRAMA EVER STAGED

THE GREATEST DRAMA EVER STAGED

IS THE OFFICIAL CREED OF CHRISTENDOM

Official Christianity, of late years, has been having what is known as "a bad press." We are constantly assured that the churches are empty because preachers insist too much upon doctrine—"dull dogma," as people call it. The fact is the precise opposite. It is the neglect of dogma that makes for dullness. The Christian faith is the most exciting drama that ever staggered the imagination of man—and the dogma is the drama.

That drama is summarised quite clearly in the creeds of the Church, and if we think it dull it is because we either have never really read those amazing documents, or have recited them so often and so mechanically as to have lost all sense of their meaning. The plot pivots upon a single character, and the whole action is the answer to a single central problem: *What think ye of Christ?* Before we adopt any of the unofficial solutions (some of which are indeed excessively dull)— before we dismiss Christ as a myth, an idealist, a demagogue, a liar or a lunatic—it will do no harm to find out what the creeds really say about Him. What does the Church think of Christ?

The Church's answer is categorical and uncompromising, and it is this: That Jesus Bar-Joseph, the carpenter of Nazareth, was in fact and in truth, and in the most exact and literal sense of the words, the God "by Whom all things were made." His body and brain were those of a common man; His personality was the personality of God, so far as that personality could be expressed in human terms. He was not a kind of dæmon or fairy pretending to be human; He was in every respect a genuine living man. He was not merely a man so good as to be "like God"—He *was* God.

Now, this is not just a pious commonplace; it is not common-place at all. For what it means is this, among other things: that for whatever reason God chose to make man as he is—limited and suffer-ing and subject to sorrows and death—He had the honesty and the courage to take His own medicine. Whatever game He is playing with His creation, He has kept His own rules and played fair. He can exact nothing from man that He has not exacted from Himself. He has Him-self gone through the whole of human experience, from the trivial irri-tations of family life and the cramping restrictions of hard work and lack of money to the worst horrors of pain and humiliation, defeat, despair and death. When He was a man, He played the man. He was born in poverty and died in disgrace and thought it well worth while.

Christianity is, of course, not the only religion that has found the best explanation of human life in the idea of an incarnate and suf-fering god. The Egyptian Osiris died and rose again; Æschylus in his play, *The Eumenides*, reconciled man to God by the theory of a suffer-ing Zeus. But in most theologies, the god is supposed to have suffered and died in some remote and mythical period of pre-history. The Christian story, on the other hand, starts off briskly in St. Matthew's account with a place and a date: "When Jesus was born in Bethlehem of Judæa in the days of Herod the King." St. Luke, still more practical-ly and prosaically, pins the thing down by a reference to a piece of government finance. God, he says, was made man in the year when Cæsar Augustus was taking a census in connection with a scheme of taxation. Similarly, we might date an event by saying that it took place in the year that Great Britain went off the gold standard. About thirty-three years later (we are informed) God was executed, for being a po-litical nuisance, "under Pontius Pilate "—much as we might say, "when Mr. Joynson-Hicks was Home Secretary." It is as definite and concrete as all that.

Possibly we might prefer not to take this tale too seriously—there are disquieting points about it. Here we had a man of Divine cha-racter walking and talking among us—and what did we find to do with Him? The common people, indeed, "heard Him gladly"; but our lead-ing authorities in Church and State considered that He talked too much and uttered too many disconcerting truths. So we bribed one of His friends to hand Him over quietly to the police, and we tried Him on a rather vague charge of creating a disturbance, and had Him publicly flogged and hanged on the common gallows, "thanking God we were rid of a knave." All this was not very creditable to us, even if He was (as many people thought and think) only a harmless crazy preacher. But if the Church is right about Him, it was more discreditable still ; for the man we hanged was God Almighty.

So that is the outline of the official story—the tale of the time when God was the under-dog and got beaten, when He submitted to the conditions He had laid down and became a man like the men He had made, and the men He had made broke Him and killed Him. This is the dogma we find so dull—this terrifying drama of which God is the victim and hero.

If this is dull, then what, in Heaven's name, is worthy to be called exciting? The people who hanged Christ never, to do them justice, accused Him of being a bore—on the contrary; they thought Him too dynamic to be safe. It has been left for later generations to muffle up that shattering personality and surround Him with an atmosphere of tedium. We have very efficiently pared the claws of the Lion of Judah, certified Him "meek and mild," and recommended Him as a fitting household pet for pale curates and pious old ladies. To those who knew Him, however, He in no way suggested a milk-and-water person; *they* objected to Him as a dangerous firebrand. True, He was tender to the unfortunate, patient with honest inquirers and humble before Heaven; but He insulted respectable clergymen by calling them hypocrites; He referred to King Herod as "that fox"; He went to parties in disreputable company and was looked upon as a "gluttonous man and a wine-bibber, a friend of publicans and sinners"; He assaulted indignant tradesmen and threw them and their belongings out of the Temple; He drove a coach-and-horses through a number of sacrosanct and hoary regulations; He cured diseases by any means that came handy, with a shocking casualness in the matter of other people's pigs and property; He showed no proper deference for wealth or social position; when confronted with neat dialectical traps, He displayed a paradoxical humour that affronted serious-minded people, and He retorted by asking disagreeably searching questions that could not be answered by rule of thumb. He was emphatically not a dull man in His human lifetime, and if He was God, there can be nothing dull about God either. But He had "a daily beauty in His life that made us ugly," and officialdom felt that the established order of things would be more secure without Him. So they did away with God in the name of peace and quietness.

"And the third day He rose again"; what are we to make of that? One thing is certain: if He was God and nothing else, His immortality means nothing to us; if He was man and no more, His death is no more important than yours or mine. But if He really was both God and man, then when the man Jesus died, God died too, and when the God Jesus rose from the dead, man rose too, because they were one and the same person. The Church binds us to no theory about the exact composition of Christ's Resurrection Body. A body of some kind there had to be, since man cannot perceive the Infinite otherwise than in terms of space and time. It may have been made from the same elements as the body that disappeared so strangely from the guarded tomb, but it was not that old, limited, mortal body, though it was recognisably like it. In any case, those who saw the risen Christ remained persuaded that life was worth living and death a triviality—an attitude curiously unlike that of the modern defeatist, who is firmly persuaded that life is a disaster and death (rather inconsistently) a major catastrophe.

Now, nobody is compelled to believe a single word of this remarkable story. God (says the Church) has created us perfectly free to disbelieve in Him as much as we choose. If we do disbelieve, then He and we must take the consequences in a world ruled by cause and effect. The Church says further, that man did, in fact, disbelieve, and that God did, in fact, take the consequences. All the same, if we are going to disbelieve a thing, it seems on the whole to be desirable that we should first find out what, exactly, we are disbelieving. Very well, then: "The right Faith is, that we believe that Jesus Christ is God and Man. Perfect God and perfect Man, of a reasonable soul and human flesh subsisting. Who although He be God and Man, yet is He not two, but one Christ." There is the essential doctrine, of which the whole elaborate structure of Christian faith and morals is only the logical consequence.

Now, we may call that doctrine exhilarating or we may call it devastating; we may call it revelation or we may call it rubbish; but if we call it dull, then words have no meaning at all. That God should play the tyrant over man is a dismal story of unrelieved oppression; that man should play the tyrant over man is the usual dreary record of human futility; but that man should play the tyrant over God and find Him a better man than himself is an astonishing drama indeed. Any journalist, hearing of it for the first time, would recognise it as News; those who did hear it for the first time actually called it News, and good news at that; though we are apt to forget that the word Gospel ever meant anything so sensational.

Perhaps the drama is played out now, and Jesus is safely dead and buried. Perhaps. It is ironical and entertaining to consider that once at least in the world's history those words might have been spoken with complete conviction, and that was upon the eve of the Resurrection

THE TRIUMPH OF EASTER

"*O FELIX CULPA!*" said Augustine of Hippo, rather dangerously, with reference to the sin of Adam. "O happy guilt, that did deserve such and so great a Redeemer!"

It is difficult, perhaps, to imagine a pronouncement that lays itself more open to misunderstanding. It is the kind of paradox that bishops and clergy are warned to beware of uttering from the pulpit. But, then, the Bishop of Hippo was a very remarkable bishop indeed, with a courage of his convictions rare in highly-placed ecclesiastical persons.

If spiritual pastors are to refrain from saying anything that might ever, by any possibility, be misunderstood by anybody, they will end—as in fact many of them do—by never saying anything worth hearing. Incidentally, this particular brand of timidity is the besetting sin of the good churchman. Not that the Church approves it. She knows it of old for a part of the great, sprawling, drowsy, deadly Sin of Sloth—a sin from which the preachers of fads, schisms, heresies and anti-Christ are most laudably free.

The children of this world are not only (as Christ so caustically observed) wiser in their generation than the children of light; they are also more energetic, more stimulating and bolder. It is always, of course, more amusing to attack than to defend; but good Christian people should have learnt by now that it is best to defend by attacking, seeing that the Kingdom of Heaven suffereth violence, and the violent take it by force. St. Augustine, anyway, seeing the perpetual problem of sin and evil being brought up and planted, like a battery, against the Christian position, sallied promptly forth, like the good strategist he was, and spiked its guns with a thanksgiving.

The problem of sin and evil is, as everybody knows, one which all religions have to face, especially those that postulate an all-good and all-powerful God. "If," we say readily, "God is holy and omnipotent, He would interfere and stop all this kind of thing"—meaning by "this kind of thing" wars, persecutions, cruelties, Hitlerism, Bolshevism, or whatever large issue happens to be distressing our minds at the time. But let us be quite sure that we have really considered the problem in all its aspects.

"Why doesn't God smite this dictator dead?" is a question a little remote from us. Why, madam, did He not strike you dumb and imbecile before you uttered that baseless and unkind slander the day before yesterday? Or me, before I behaved with such cruel lack of consideration to that well-meaning friend? And why, sir, did He not cause your hand to rot off at the wrist before you signed your name to that dirty little bit of financial trickery?

You did not quite mean that? But why not? Your misdeeds and mine are none the less repellent because our opportunities for doing damage are less spectacular than those of some other people. Do you suggest that your doings and mine are too trivial for God to bother about? That cuts both ways; for, in that case, it would make precious little difference to His creation if He wiped us both out to-morrow.

Well, perhaps that is not quite what we meant. We meant why did God create His universe on these lines at all? Why did He not make us mere puppets, incapable of executing anything but His own pattern of perfection? Some schools of thought assert that He did, that everything we do (including Jew-baiting in Germany and our own disgusting rudeness to Aunt Eliza) is rigidly determined for us, and that, however much we may dislike the pattern, we can do nothing about it. This is one of those theories that are supposed to free us from the trammels of superstition. It certainly relieves our minds of all responsibility; unfortunately, it imposes a fresh set of trammels of its own. Also, however much we may believe in it, we seem forced to behave as though we did not.

Christians (surprising as it may appear) are not the only people who fail to act up to their creed; for what determinist philosopher, when his breakfast bacon is uneatable, will not blame the free will of the cook, like any Christian? To be sure, the philosopher's protest, like his bacon, is pre-determined also; that is the silly part of it. Our minds are the material we have to work upon when constructing philosophies, and it seems but an illogical creed, whose proof depends on our discarding all the available evidence.

The Church, at any rate, says that man's will is free, and that evil is the price we pay for knowledge, particularly the kind of knowledge which we call self-consciousness. It follows that we can, by God's grace, do something about the pattern. Moreover, God Himself, says the Church, is doing something about it—with our co-operation, if we choose, in despite of us if we refuse to co-operate—but always, steadily, working the pattern out.

And here we come up against the ultimate question which no theology, no philosophy, no theory of the universe has ever so much as attempted to answer completely. Why should God, if there is a God, create anything, at any time, of any kind at all? That is a real mystery, and probably the only completely insoluble mystery there is. The one person who might be able to give some sort of guess at the answer is the creative artist, and he, of all people in the world, is the least inclined even to ask the question, being accustomed to take all creative activity as its own sufficient justification.

But we may all, perhaps, allow that it is easier to believe the universe to have come into existence for some reason than for no reason at all. The Church asserts that there is a Mind which made the universe, that He made it because He is the sort of Mind that takes pleasure in creation, and that if we want to know what the Mind of the

Creator is, we must look at Christ. In Him, we shall discover a Mind that loved His own creation so completely that He became part of it, suffered with and for it, and made it a sharer in His own glory and a fellow-worker with Himself in the working out of His own design for it.

That is the bold postulate that the Church asks us to accept, adding that, if we do accept it (and every theoretical scheme demands the acceptance of some postulate or other) the answers to all our other problems will be found to make sense.

Accepting the postulate, then, and looking at Christ, what do we find God "doing about" this business of sin and evil? And what is He expecting us to do about it? Here, the Church is clear enough. We find God continually at work turning evil into good. Not, as a rule, by irrelevant miracles and theatrically effective judgments—Christ was seldom very encouraging to those who demanded signs, or lightnings from Heaven, and God is too subtle and too economical a craftsman to make very much use of those methods. But He takes our sins and errors and turns them into victories, as He made the crime of the crucifixion to be the salvation of the world. "*O felix culpa!*" exclaimed St. Augustine, contemplating the accomplished work.

Here is the place where we are exceedingly liable to run into misunderstanding. God does not need our sin, still less does He make us sin, in order to demonstrate His power and glory. His is not the uneasy power that has to reassure itself by demonstrations. Nor is it desirable that we should create evils on purpose for the fun of seeing Him put them right. That is not the idea at all. Nor yet are we to imagine that evil does not matter, since God can make it all right in the long run.

Whatever the Church preaches on this point, it is *not* a facile optimism. And it is not the advisability of doing evil that good may come. Over-simplification of this sort is as misleading as too much complication and just as perilously attractive. It is, for instance, startling and illuminating to hear a surgeon say casually, when congratulated upon some miracle of healing, "Of course, we couldn't have done that operation without the experience we gained in the War."

There is a good result of evil; but, even if the number of sufferers healed were to exceed that of all the victims who suffered in the War, does that allay the pangs of the victims or of any one of them, or excuse the guilt that makes war possible? No, says the Church, it does not. If an artist discovers that the experience gained through his worst sins enables him to produce his best work, does that entitle him to live like a beast for the sake of his art? No, says the Church, it does not. We can behave as badly as we like, but we cannot escape the consequences. "Take what you will, said God" (according to the Spanish proverb) "take it and pay for it." Or somebody else may do the paying and pay fully, willingly and magnificently, but the debt is still ours. "The Son of man goeth as it is written of Him; but woe unto that man by whom the Son of man is betrayed! it had been good for that man if he had not been born."

When Judas sinned, Jesus paid; He brought good out of evil, He led out triumph from the gates of hell and brought all mankind out with Him; but the suffering of Jesus and the sin of Judas remain a reality. God did not abolish the fact of evil: He transformed it. He did not stop the crucifixion: He rose from the dead.

"Then Judas, which had betrayed Him, when he saw that He was condemned,... cast down the pieces of silver in the temple, and departed, and went and hanged himself." And thereby Judas committed the final, the fatal, the most pitiful error of all; for he despaired of God and himself and never waited to see the Resurrection. Had he done so, there would have been an encounter, and an opportunity, to leave invention bankrupt; but unhappily for himself, he did not. In this world, at any rate, he never saw the triumph of Christ fulfilled upon him, and through him, and despite of him. He saw the dreadful payment made, and never knew what victory had been purchased with the price.

All of us, perhaps, are too ready, when our behaviour turns out to have appalling consequences, to rush out and hang ourselves. Sometimes we do worse, and show an inclination to go and hang other people. Judas, at least, seems to have blamed nobody but himself, and St. Peter, who had a minor betrayal of his own to weep for, made his act of contrition and waited to see what came next. What came next for St. Peter and the other disciples was the sudden assurance of what God was, and with it the answer to all the riddles.

If Christ could take evil and suffering and do that sort of thing with them, then of course it was all worth while, and the triumph of Easter linked up with that strange, triumphant prayer in the Upper Room, which the events of Good Friday had seemed to make so puzzling. As for their own parts in the drama, nothing could now alter the fact that they had been stupid, cowardly, faithless, and in many ways singularly unhelpful; but they did not allow any morbid and egotistical remorse to inhibit their joyful activities in the future.

Now, indeed, they could go out and "do something" about the problem of sin and suffering. They had seen the strong hands of God twist the crown of thorns into a crown of glory, and in hands as strong as that they knew themselves safe. They had misunderstood practically everything Christ had ever said to them, but no matter: the thing made sense at last, and the meaning was far beyond anything they had dreamed. They had expected a walk-over, and they beheld a victory; they had expected an earthly Messiah, and they beheld the Soul of Eternity.

It had been said to them of old time, "No man shall look upon My face and live"; but for them a means had been found. They had seen the face of the living God turned upon them; and it was the face of a suffering and rejoicing Man.

STRONG MEAT

"For every one that useth milk is unskilful in the word of righteousness; for he is a babe.
"But strong meat belongeth to them that are of full age, even those who by reason of use have their senses exercised to discern both good and evil."

—Epistle to the Hebrews

I. STRONG MEAT

II. THE DOGMA IS THE DRAMA

STRONG MEAT

It is over twenty years since I first read the words, in some forgotten book. I remember neither the name of the author, nor that of the Saint from whose meditations he was quoting. [1] Only the statement itself has survived the accidents of transmission: "*Cibus sum grandium; cresce, et manducabis Me*"—"I am the food of the full-grown; become a man, and thou shalt feed on Me."

Here is a robust assertion of the claim of Christianity to be a religion for adult minds. I am glad to think, *now*, that it impressed me so forcibly *then*, when I was still comparatively young. To protest, when one has left one's youth behind, against the prevalent assumption that there is no salvation for the middle-aged is all very well; but it is apt to provoke a mocking reference to the fox who lost his tail. One is in a stronger position if one can show that one had already registered the protest before circumstances rendered it expedient.

There is a popular school of thought (or, more strictly, of feeling) which violently resents the operation of Time upon the human spirit. It looks upon age as something between a crime and an insult. Its prophets have banished from their savage vocabulary all such words as "adult," "mature," "experienced," "venerable"; they know only snarling and sneering epithets, like "middle-aged," "elderly," "stuffy," "senile" and "decrepit." With these they flagellate that which they themselves are, or must shortly become, as though abuse were an incantation to exorcise the inexorable. Theirs is neither the thoughtless courage that "makes mouths at the invisible event," nor the reasoned courage that foresees the event and endures it; still less is it the ecstatic courage that embraces and subdues the event. It is the vicious and desperate fury of a trapped beast; and it is not a pretty sight.

Such men, finding no value for the world as it is, proclaim very loudly their faith in the future, "which is in the hands of the young." With this flattery, they bind their own burden on the shoulders of the next generation. For their own failures, Time alone is to blame—not Sin, which is expiable, but Time, which is irreparable. From the relentless reality of age they seek escape into a fantasy of youth—their own or other people's. First love, boyhood ideals, childish dreams, the song at the mother's breast, the blind security of the womb—from these they construct a monstrous fabric of pretence, to be their hiding-place from the tempest. Their faith is not really in the future, but in the past. Paradoxical as it may seem, to believe in youth is to look backward; to look forward, we must believe in age. "Except," said Christ, "ye become as little children"—and the words are sometimes quoted to justify the flight into infantilism. Now, children differ in many ways, but they have one thing in common. Peter Pan— if indeed he exists otherwise than in the nostalgic imagination of an adult—is a case for the pathologist. All normal children (however much we discourage them) look forward to growing up. "Except ye become as little children," except you can wake on your fiftieth birthday with the same forward-looking excitement and interest in life that you enjoyed when you were five, "ye cannot see the Kingdom of God." One must not only die daily, but every day one must be born again.

"How can a man be born when he is old?" asked Nicodemus. His question has been ridiculed; but it is very reasonable and even profound. "Can he enter a second time into his mother's womb and be born?" Can he escape from Time, creep back into the comfortable pre-natal darkness, renounce the values of experience ? The answer makes short work of all such fantasies. "That which is born of the flesh is flesh, and that which is born of the Spirit is spirit." The spirit alone is eternal youth; the mind and the body must learn to make terms with Time.

Time is a difficult subject for thought, because in a sense we know too much about it. It is perhaps the only phenomenon of which we have direct apprehension; if all our senses were destroyed, we should still remain aware of duration. Moreover, all conscious thought is a process in time; so that to think consciously about Time is like trying to use a foot-rule to measure its own length. The awareness of timelessness, which some people have, does not belong to the order of conscious thought and cannot be directly expressed in the language of conscious thought, which is temporal. For every conscious human purpose (including thought) we are compelled to reckon (in every sense of the word) with Time.

Now, the Christian Church has always taken a thoroughly realistic view of Time, and has been very particular to distinguish between Time and Eternity. In her view of the matter, Time is not an aspect or a fragment of Eternity, nor is Eternity an endless extension of Time; the two concepts belong to different categories. Both have a divine reality: God is the Ancient of Days and also the I AM: the Everlasting, and also the Eternal Present; the Logos and also the Father; the Creeds, with their usual practicality, issue a sharp warning that we shall get into a nasty mess if we confuse the two or deny the reality of either. Moreover, the mystics—those rare spirits who are simultaneously aware of Time and Eternity—support the doctrine by their knowledge and example. They are never vague, woolly-minded people to whom Time means nothing; on the contrary, they insist more than anybody upon the validity of Time and the actuality of human experience.

The reality of Time is not affected by considering it as a dimension in a space-time continuum or as a solid having dimensions of its own. "There's a great devil in the universe," says Kay in *Time and the Conways*, "and we call it Time.... If things were merely mixed—good and bad—that would be all right, but they get worse.... Time's beating us." Her brother replies that Time is "only a kind of dream," and that the "happy young Conways of the past" are still real and existing. "We're seeing another bit of the view—a bad bit if you like—but the whole landscape's still there.... At this moment, or any moment, we're only a cross-section of our real selves. What we *really* are is the whole stretch of ourselves, all our time, and when we come to the end of this life, all our time will be *us*—the real you, the real me."

Granted all this—that the happy young Conways still co-exist, *now*, with the unhappy, middle-aged Conways; granted also the converse—that the unhappy, middle-aged Conways already co-existed, *then*, with the happy young Conways. What of it? All we have done is to substitute a spatial image for a temporal one. Instead of a *progress* from good to evil we have a *prospect* (or "landscape") of mixed good and evil, which, viewed in its entirety ("when we come to the end of this life") must necessarily contain more evil than good, since things "get worse and worse." Kay may find this "all right"; the fact remains that there is here no conquest over Time, but an unconditional surrender.

That surrender is made in the moment when we assume that Time is evil in itself and brings nothing but deterioration. It is a pity that the Conway family contained no saint, no artist, no one who had achieved any measure of triumphant fulfilment. His opinion would have been of great interest, since he might have spoken with authority of the soul's development in Time, of the vigorous grappling with evil that transforms it into good, of the dark night of the soul that precedes crucifixion and issues in resurrection.

In contending with the problem of evil it is useless to try to escape either *from* the bad past or *into* the good past. The only way to deal with the past is to accept the whole past, and by accepting it, to change its meaning. The hero of T. S. Eliot's *The Family Reunion*, haunted by the guilt of a hereditary evil, seeks at first "To creep back through the little door" into the shelter of the unaltered past, and finds no refuge there from the pursuing hounds of heaven. "Now I know That the last apparent refuge, the safe shelter, That is where one meets them; that is the way of spectres...." So long as he flees from Time and Evil he is thrall to them, not till he welcomes them does he find strength to transmute them. "And now I know That my business is not to run away, but to pursue, Not to avoid being found, but to seek.... It is at once the hardest thing, and the only thing possible. Now they will lead me; I shall be safe with them. I am not safe here.... I must follow the bright angels." Then, and only then, is he enabled to apprehend the good in the evil and to see the terrible hunters of the soul in their true angelic shape. "I feel quite happy, as if happiness Did not consist in getting what one wanted, Or in getting rid of what can't be got rid of, But in a different vision." It is the release, not from, but into, Reality.

This is the great way of Christian acceptance—a very different thing from so-called "Christian" resignation, which merely submits without ecstasy. "Repentance," says a Christian writer [2], "is no more than a passionate intention to know all things after the mode of Heaven, and it is impossible to know evil as good if you insist on knowing it as evil." For man's evil knowledge, "there could be but one perfect remedy—to know the evil of the past itself as good, and to be free from the necessity of evil in the future—to find right knowledge and perfect freedom together; to know all things as occasions of love."

The story of Passion-Tide and Easter is the story of the winning of that freedom and of that victory over the evils of Time. The burden of the guilt is accepted ("He was made Sin") the last agony of alienation from God is passed through (*Eloi, lama sabachthani*); the temporal Body is broken and remade; and Time and Eternity are reconciled in a Single Person. There is no retreat here to the Paradise of primal ignorance; the new Kingdom of God is built upon the foundations of spiritual experience. Time is not denied; it is fulfilled. "I am the food of the full-grown."

THE DOGMA IS THE DRAMA

"Any stigma," said a witty tongue, "will do to beat a dogma"; and the flails of ridicule have been brandished with such energy of late on the threshing-floor of controversy that the true seed of the Word has become well-nigh lost amid the whirling of chaff. Christ, in His Divine innocence, said to the Woman of Samaria, "Ye worship ye know not what"—being apparently under the impression that it might be desirable, on the whole, to know what one was worshipping. He thus showed Himself sadly out of touch with the twentieth-century mind, for the cry to-day is: "Away with the tedious complexities of dogma—let us have the simple spirit of worship; just worship, no matter of what!" The only drawback to this demand for a generalised and undirected worship is the practical difficulty of arousing any sort of enthusiasm for the worship of nothing in particular.

It would not perhaps be altogether surprising if, in this nominally Christian country, where the Creeds are daily recited, there were a number of people who knew all about Christian doctrine and disliked it. It is more startling to discover how many people there are who heartily dislike and despise Christianity without having the faintest notion what it is. If you tell them, they cannot believe you. I do not mean that they cannot believe the doctrine: that would be understandable enough, since it takes some believing. I mean that they simply cannot believe that anything so interesting, so exciting and so dramatic can be the orthodox Creed of the Church.

That this is really the case was made plain to me by the questions asked me, mostly by young men, about my Canterbury play, THE ZEAL OF THY HOUSE. The action of the play involves a dramatic presentation of a few fundamental Christian dogmas—in particular, the application to human affairs of the doctrine of the Incarnation. That the Church believed Christ to be in any *real* sense God, or that the Eternal Word was supposed to be associated in any way with the work of Creation; that Christ was held to be at the same time Man in any *real* sense of the word; that the doctrine of the Trinity could be considered to have any relation to fact or any bearing on psychological truth; that the Church considered Pride to be sinful, or indeed took notice of any sin beyond the more disreputable sins of the flesh:—all these things were looked upon as astonishing and revolutionary novelties, imported into the Faith by the feverish imagination of a playwright. I protested in vain against this flattering tribute to my powers of invention, referring my inquirers to the Creeds, to the Gospels and to the offices of the Church; I insisted that if my play was dramatic it was so, not in spite of the dogma but because of it—that, in short, the dogma *was* the drama. The explanation was, however, not well received; it was felt that if there was anything attractive in Christian philosophy I must have put it there myself.

Judging by what my young friends tell me and also by what is said on the subject in anti-Christian literature written by people who ought to have taken a little trouble to find out what they are attacking before attacking it, I have come to the conclusion that a short examination paper on the Christian religion might be very generally answered as follows:

Q.: What does the Church think of God the Father?

A.: He is omnipotent and holy. He created the world and imposed on man conditions impossible of fulfilment; He is very angry if these are not carried out. He sometimes interferes by means of arbitrary judgments and miracles, distributed with a good deal of favouritism. He likes to be truckled to and is always ready to pounce on anybody who trips up over a difficulty in the Law, or is having a bit of fun. He is rather like a Dictator, only larger and more arbitrary.

Q.: What does the Church think of God the Son?

A.: He is in some way to be identified with Jesus of Nazareth. It was not His fault that the world was made like this, and, unlike God the Father, He is friendly to man and did His best to reconcile man to God (see *Atonement*). He has a good deal of influence with God, and if you want anything done, it is best to apply to Him.

Q.: What does the Church think of God the Holy Ghost?

A.: I don't know exactly. He was never seen or heard of till Whit-Sunday. There is a sin against Him which damns you for ever, but nobody knows what it is.

Q.: What is the doctrine of the Trinity?

A.: "The Father incomprehensible, the Son incomprehensible, and the whole thing incomprehensible." Something put in by theologians to make it more difficult—nothing to do with daily life or ethics.

Q.: What was Jesus Christ like in real life?

A.: He was a good man—so good as to be called the Son of God. He is to be identified in some way with God the Son (q.v.). He was meek and mild and preached a simple religion of love and pacifism. He had no sense of humour. Anything in the Bible that suggests another side to His character must be an interpolation, or a paradox invented by G. K. Chesterton. If we try to live like Him, God the Father will let us off being damned hereafter and only have us tortured in this life instead.

Q.: What is meant by the Atonement?

A.: God wanted to damn everybody, but His vindictive sadism was sated by the crucifixion of His own Son, who was quite innocent, and therefore a particularly attractive victim. He now only damns people who don't follow Christ or who never heard of Him.

Q.: What does the Church think of sex?

A.: God made it necessary to the machinery of the world, and tolerates it, provided the parties (a) are married, and (b) get no pleasure out of it.

Q.: What does the Church call Sin?

A.: Sex (otherwise than as excepted above); getting drunk; saying "damn"; murder, and cruelty to dumb animals; not going to church; most kinds of amusement. "Original sin" means that anything we enjoy doing is wrong.

Q.: What is faith?

A.: Resolutely shutting your eyes to scientific fact.

Q.: What is the human intellect?

A.: A barrier to faith.

Q.: What are the seven Christian virtues?

A.: Respectability; childishness; mental timidity; dulness; sentimentality; censoriousness; and depression of spirits.

Q.: Wilt thou be baptised in this faith?

A.: No fear!

I cannot help feeling that as a statement of Christian orthodoxy, these replies are inadequate, if not misleading. But I also cannot help feeling that they do fairly accurately represent what many people take Christian orthodoxy to be, and for this state of affairs I am inclined to blame the orthodox. Whenever an average Christian is represented in a novel or a play, he is pretty sure to be shown practising one or all of the Seven Deadly Virtues enumerated above, and I am afraid that this is the impression made by the average Christian upon the world at large.

Perhaps we are not following Christ all the way or in quite the right spirit. We are apt, for example, to be a little sparing of the palms and the hosannas. We are chary of wielding the scourge of small cords, lest we should offend somebody or interfere with trade. We do not furbish up our wits to disentangle knotty questions about Sunday observance and tribute-money, nor hasten to sit at the feet of the doctors, both hearing them and asking them questions. We pass hastily over disquieting jests about making friends with the mammon of unrighteousness and alarming observations about bringing not peace but a sword; nor do we distinguish ourselves by the graciousness with which we sit at meat with publicans and sinners. Somehow or other, and with the best intentions, we have shown the world the typical Christian in the likeness of a crashing and rather ill-natured bore—and this in the Name of One Who assuredly never bored a soul in those thirty-three years during which He passed through the world like a flame.

Let us, in Heaven's name, drag out the Divine Drama from under the dreadful accumulation of slip-shod thinking and trashy sentiment heaped upon it, and set it on an open stage to startle the world into some sort of vigorous reaction. If the pious are the first to be shocked, so much the worse for the pious—others will pass into the Kingdom of Heaven before them. If all men are offended because of Christ, let them be offended; but where is the sense of their being offended at something that is not Christ and is nothing like Him? We do Him singularly little honour by watering down His personality till it could not offend a fly. Surely it is not the business of the Church to adapt Christ to men, but to adapt men to Christ.

It is the dogma that is the drama—not beautiful phrases, nor comforting sentiments, nor vague aspirations to loving-kindness and uplift, nor the promise of something nice after death—but the terrifying assertion that the same God Who made the world lived in the world and passed through the grave and gate of death. Show that to the

81

heathen, and they may not believe it; but at least they may realise that here is something that a man might be glad to believe.

[Footnote 1] But I would have laid any odds, from the style, that it was Augustine of Hippo; and so, indeed, it proves to be (*Confessions*: vii.10).

[Footnote 2] Charles Williams: *He Came Down from Heaven.*

Also from Benediction Books ...
Wandering Between Two Worlds: Essays on Faith and Art
Anita Mathias
Benediction Books, 2007
152 pages
ISBN: 0955373700

Available from www.amazon.com, www.amazon.co.uk

In these wide-ranging lyrical essays, Anita Mathias writes, in lush, lovely prose, of her naughty Catholic childhood in Jamshedpur, India; her large, eccentric family in Mangalore, a sea-coast town converted by the Portuguese in the sixteenth century; her rebellion and atheism as a teenager in her Himalayan boarding school, run by German missionary nuns, St. Mary's Convent, Nainital; and her abrupt religious conversion after which she entered Mother Teresa's convent in Calcutta as a novice. Later rich, elegant essays explore the dualities of her life as a writer, mother, and Christian in the United States-- Domesticity and Art, Writing and Prayer, and the experience of being "an alien and stranger" as an immigrant in America, sensing the need for roots.

About the Author

Anita Mathias is the author of *Wandering Between Two Worlds: Essays on Faith and Art.* She has a B.A. and M.A. in English from Somerville College, Oxford University, and an M.A. in Creative Writing from the Ohio State University, USA. Anita won a National Endowment of the Arts fellowship in Creative Nonfiction in 1997. She lives in Oxford, England with her husband, Roy, and her daughters, Zoe and Irene.

Visit Anita's website
    http://www.anitamathias.com,
and Anita's blog
    http://theoxfordchristian.blogspot.com, (Dreaming Beneath the Spires)

The Church That Had Too Much
Anita Mathias
Benediction Books, 2010
52 pages
ISBN: 9781849026567

Available from www.amazon.com, www.amazon.co.uk

The Church That Had Too Much was very well-intentioned. She
wanted to love God, she wanted to love people, but she was both
hampered by her muchness and the abundance of her posses-
sions, and beset by ambition, power struggles and snobbery.
Read about the surprising way The Church That Had Too Much
began to resolve her problems in this deceptively simple and
enchanting fable.

About the Author

Anita Mathias is the author of *Wandering Between Two Worlds:
Essays on Faith and Art.* She has a B.A. and M.A. in English
from Somerville College, Oxford University, and an M.A. in
Creative Writing from the Ohio State University, USA. Anita
won a National Endowment of the Arts fellowship in Creative
Nonfiction in 1997. She lives in Oxford, England with her hus-
band, Roy, and her daughters, Zoe and Irene.

Visit Anita at http://www.anitamathias.com, and on
http://theoxfordchristian.blogspot.com, her Christian blog;
http://wanderingbetweentwoworlds.blogspot.com/, her personal blog, and
http://thegoodbooksblog.blogspot.com, her literary and writing blog.

www.ingramcontent.com/pod-product-compliance
Lightning Source LLC
Chambersburg PA
CBHW030519100426
42813CB00001B/87